SUPER STRUCTURES OF THE WORLD

INTERNATIONAL SPACE STATION

BLACKBIRCH®
PRESS

THOMSON
GALE

San Diego • Detroit • New York • San Francisco • Cleveland • New Haven, Conn. • Waterville, Maine • London • Munich

THOMSON

GALE

For more information, contact
The Gale Group, Inc.
27500 Drake Rd.
Farmington Hills, MI 48331-3535
Or you can visit our Internet site at http://www.gale.com

LIBRARY OF CONGRESS CATALOGING-IN-PUBLICATION DATA

International space station / Elaine Pascoe, book editor.
      p. cm. — (Super structures of the world)
Summary: Examines the history of cooperation between Russia, the United States, and
other countries to built and maintain the space station
Includes bibliographical references and index.
   ISBN 1-56711-865-8 (hardback : alk. paper) ISBN 1-41030-189-3 (pbk : alk. paper)
   1. Space stations—Russia-United States—Juvenile literature. 2. Space-Untied States—
Russia—Design and construction—Juvenile literature. [1. Space-United States—Russia.] I.
Pascoe, Elaine. II. Series.

TL797.P76 2004
388.4'28'09421—dc21

Printed in China
10 9 8 7 6 5 4 3 2 1

INTERNATIONAL SPACE STATION

Space, an infinite void without air or water, where nothing can survive—until now. Humans are building a super structure in space. It's the most dangerous construction project ever attempted—and the hardest.

Someday, this structure will help us go to Mars, and it will push our minds and bodies to the edge. It's the International Space Station.

November 20, 1998

At the Baikonur Cosmodrome, Kazakstan, a gigantic proton rocket, blasts into space carrying a 20-ton aluminum cylinder called Zarya, Russian for "sunrise." Russian scientists watch with hope and exhilaration. They are not alone.

December 3, 1998

Two weeks later, the shuttle Endeavour *blasts off from the Kennedy Space Center Cape Canaveral, carrying a 12-ton module named Unity. Now, 240 miles above Earth, the* Endeavour's *crew will attempt to join* Unity *with Zarya, as they race around the planet together at 17,000 miles per hour. It is the dawn of a new era of space technology and international cooperation.*

The International Space Station began by joining the payloads of an American space shuttle (right) with a Russian proton rocket (inset).

For nearly half a century, Russians and Americans were bitter rivals in a race to conquer space. Yet, they enter a new millennium as partners in the most ambitious construction project ever attempted, the International Space Station.

The two modules launched in 1998 are only the first 2 percent of this super structure. When it's finished, the space station will be over 300 feet wide and nearly 300 feet long. In space, it will be weightless; but in Earth's gravity, it would weigh over a million pounds. Thirty-four shuttle missions and nine Russian rocket launches will lift its one hundred components into space. It will take years to assemble them.

The space station will be a living laboratory of humankind's most daring experiment, the quest to live in the most hostile environment imaginable—the infinite, airless, lifeless void of space. No one country could build the space station alone. Its enormous size, complexity, and cost demand a level of international cooperation never attempted before.

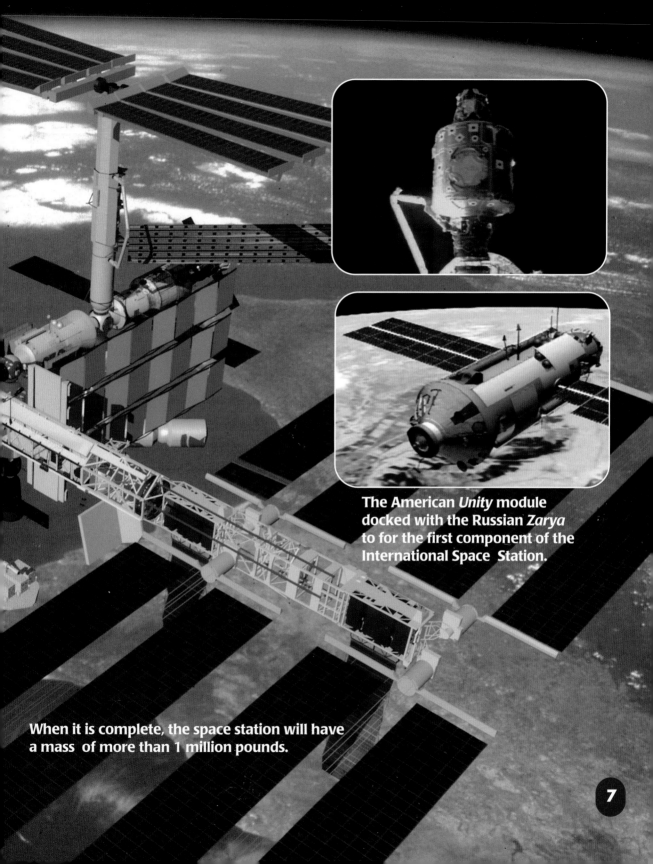

The American *Unity* module docked with the Russian *Zarya* to for the first component of the International Space Station.

When it is complete, the space station will have a mass of more than 1 million pounds.

The space station's components are being manufactured in sixteen countries—Russia, Japan, Canada, Brazil, the United States, and several European nations. In each of these countries, workers must follow identical standards in every detail, from the thickness of the steel down to every nut and bolt. If they don't, the space station modules won't fit together, and the vast undertaking will fail.

It's a daring roll of the high-tech dice, says Daniel S. Goldin, chief administrator of the National Aeronautics and Space Administration (NASA): "The first time it'll all come together is in orbit. It's so big that you can't pre-assemble it on the ground, so we'll only know whether it works when we get it out in space." As its name implies, America's

Unity is the unifying lynch-pin of the enormous structure, connecting *Zarya*, the station's control module, with American, European, and Japanese modules where space station crews will live and conduct experiments.

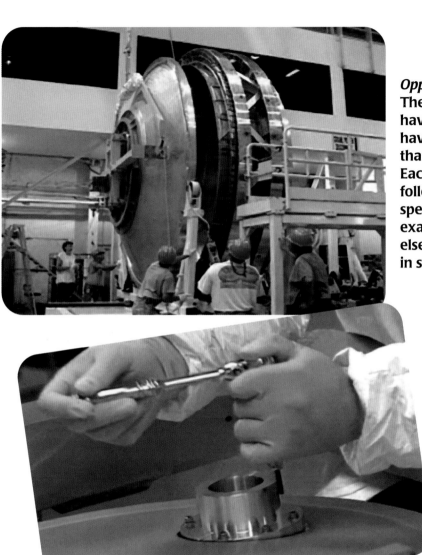

Opposite page and left:
The *Unity* module will have components that have been built in more than sixteen countries. Each country must follow manufacturing specifications that are exactly the same, or else the final assembly in space will fail.

Six astronauts, five Americans and one Russian, trained more than two years to build the first phase of the space station. All had exceptional careers as aviators, scientists, and engineers. Most had already flown hundreds of hours in space. In December 1998, they began the most difficult construction project ever attempted.

Right: The *Endeavour* crew trained for years to get read for their mission. *Below:* The *Endeavour* gets ready to launch, November 20, 1998.

Right: Members of the crew (from left), pilot W. Rick Sturckow; mission specialist Nancy J. Currie; mission commander Robert D. Cabana; and mission specialist James H. Newman pose in front of a huge module before it is readied for transport.

DECEMBER 5, 1998

Two days after launch, Endeavour's *mission begins with an incredible challenge. Using the shuttle's 50-foot-long robotic arm, astronaut Nancy Currie must grab the* Unity *module, gingerly maneuver it out of the shuttle's cargo bay, and reposition it within a few inches of a coupling device on the* Endeavour. *The* Unity *has a mass of 25,000 pounds. The shuttle's arm has never moved anything so big. But Currie succeeds, moving* Unity *into perfect position.* Endeavour's *commander, Robert D. Cabana, fires thrusters to propel the module into a docking ring, creating an airtight connection between* Unity *and the shuttle.*

The next day, Nancy Currie readies the robotic arm for a bigger challenge: Zarya. *Although it's weightless in space,* Zarya's *mass is 43,000 pounds. If it hits* Endeavour, *it could destroy the shuttle. And there's a catch:* Unity *blocks Currie's view of the Russian spacecraft. But NASA engineers have designed an ingenious solution, the computerized SVS, or space vision system. With the help of SVS, Currie maneuvers the giant arm slowly toward its target.* Endeavour's *thrusters fire, and* Unity *and* Zarya *lock together.*

This illustration shows the *Unity* module, attached to the *Endeavour*, and *Zarya* craft that needed to be docked.

Above: Nancy Currie uses a robotic arm and NASA's SVS system (middle) to connect *Unity* to *Zarya* (bottom).

Some parts of the station will be bigger than anything the space shuttle's arm can handle. Two gigantic trusses (supports) will form the completed station's backbone, supporting enormous solar panels, which will generate the station's electrical power. These components will require the biggest robot arm ever constructed.

Built in Canada, the new arm has an ingenious design that solves one of the space station's toughest problems: Where do you position the robot arm so it can reach any point on a station the size of two football fields? Like an enormous inchworm, the arm will move itself to wherever it's needed, attaching and detaching itself as it goes. Its state-of-the-art robotic hand will perform delicate tasks no other robot hand can do.

But amazing as it is, the robot arm is not the most

Above and right: **The huge robotic arm is critical in the assembly of gigantic trusses designed to hold the solar panels that provide power to the station.**

Years of safety training were needed before the space station program was actually a reality. Here, astronauts do an in-space rehearsal of a rescue with some brand new hardware.

Inset: The *Endeavour*, 250 miles above Earth.

important element in building the International Space Station. That element is human skill and courage. The teams assembling the space station are the first construction workers in outer space, working nearly 250 miles above Earth, in the most lethal environment in existence.

December 7, 1998

Joined together, the Unity and Zarya modules, nucleus of the International Space Station, orbit together 240 miles above Earth. Now begins the most dangerous work of all. The two modules must be wired together, so their electrical power and computers can be turned on.

Top: An astronaut works on *Unity* while in orbit.

Above: *Zarya* and *Unity* are locked together.

On Earth, this would be a simple task. But in space, it requires cutting-edge technology, years of training, and nerves of steel. Astronauts Jim Newman and Jerry Ross must leave the safety of the Endeavour's cabin and walk in space. The astronauts make it sound routine. Says Newman, "A space walk looks 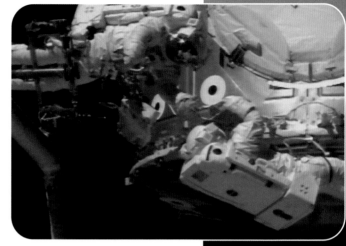 *very exciting, but a lot of what we're doing is basic construction and some grunt work."*

Grunt work it may be, but what would be routine accidents on Earth mean almost certain death in space. A tear in an astronaut's pressurized suit brings instant suffocation. A dropped tool orbiting Earth at 17,000 miles an hour can smash into the space station and damage it. And outside Earth's atmosphere, space walkers are exposed to temperatures no unprotected human could survive.

Working in space is extremely dangerous. One mistake could mean death or serious damage to the space station.

On one side of the space station, with the sun shining, temperatures can be over 200 degrees Fahrenheit; on the other side, minus 200 degrees Fahrenheit.

The space shuttle carries over one hundred tools to help the station builders. Among them are torqueless drills and liquid-filled hammers, which won't recoil in microgravity. But bringing tools to space is one thing. Using them there is another. Phil West of the Johnson Space Center explains: "If you drive a screw into a wall in your house, it

works out fine because gravity holds your feet to the floor and you're anchored there. But if an astronaut floats up to a bolt on the space station and tries to turn

Above and right: **Special tools, like this torqueless drills must be used for work in space.**

the bolt, the bolt's not going to go anywhere. The astronaut's just going to spin around the bolt—which is fun for a while, but not very productive. So you've got to find a way to anchor yourself to the spacecraft."

To solve this problem, NASA engineers created foot anchors to hold astronauts in place while they build the space station. They also invented a special device to prevent tools from winding up in orbit, and clips, pins, and tethers that prevent tools from drifting off into space if they're dropped.

NASA engineers developed foot anchors to hold astronauts in place while they work.

To train its space station builders, NASA created a microgravity construction zone on Earth. NASA's Neutral Buoyancy Lab is the largest swimming pool in the world, it holds 6.2 million gallons of water! Submerged in its near-weightlessness, astronauts can practice every step of the space station's construction. NASA also simulates space by using virtual reality. The Johnson Space Center's Virtual Reality Lab allows astronauts to get used to the feeling of floating and turning freely, without any sense of up or down.

To enable astronauts to practice assemblies in near-weightlessness, NASA built the largest swimming pool in the world.

Below: Assembly practice on a simulated module.

An astronaut trains in NASA's Virtual Reality Lab.

The station builders will also get help from a strange device that looks like a basketball and seems right out of science fiction. It's called the air-cam, a floating robot camera powered by twelve nitrogen thrusters that can move it in

any direction. The air-cam can hover over the shoulder of a space-walking crewmember, observing what the crewmember is doing. The signal can be relayed to crewmembers inside the shuttle or to experts on the ground, who can help.

But it isn't just futuristic technology that makes space construction possible. The space station's builders also owe a profound debt to the past, to a time when people first dared to live and work in space.

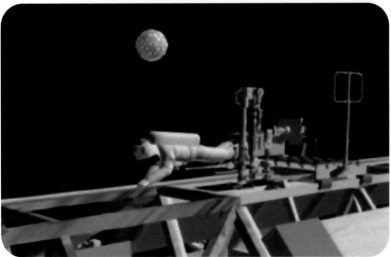

Opposite page: The basketball-shaped air-cam is a floating robot camera.

Left: Circled image shows air-cam in use on a mission.

Below: Computer illustration of how air-cam can follow astronauts working outside the space station.

The year was 1971. The United States and the Soviet Union were fiercely competing to win the space race. In that year, the Soviets launched humanity's first space habitat, a 45-foot module named *Salyut,* Russian for "salute."

Weeks later, three Soviet cosmonauts aboard a *Soyuz 10* space capsule docked with *Salyut.* The cosmonauts successfully

Top: The *Salyut* module.

Middle: The *Soyuz 10* space capsule.

Bottom: Doctors try to revive the three cosmonauts that suffocated upon re-entry.

lived on *Salyut* for three weeks. But when they returned to Earth, their triumph turned to tragedy. As *Soyuz 10* re-entered Earth's atmosphere, a hatch popped open. The spacecraft depressurized. All three cosmonauts suffocated.

On the other side of the world, NASA engineers were planning America's first space station, called *Skylab*. The *Soyuz* disaster alarmed them. So did the results of a test flight in which a monkey, sent aloft for what was to be a one-month test flight, died after eight days in orbit. There were calls for a halt to the *Skylab* program.

America weighed the risks against the importance of the mission and decided to go ahead. In 1973, NASA launched *Skylab*. But just 63 seconds into the launch, one of *Skylab's* sun shields ripped loose. The entire mission was in jeopardy.

Below left: NASA's Skylab engineers were alarmed by the Soyuz 10 disaster but launched Skylab in 1973 anyway (below).

The first team of *Skylab* astronauts, due to launch the next day, was suddenly faced with a mission never before attempted. Human beings had been space walking since 1964, but no one had ever fixed a broken vehicle in space. Astronaut Joe Kerwin, who was part of that team, recalls: "It was not yet thought feasible for people to go outside and actually repair the spacecraft. So we didn't train on the repair work that we had to do on the very first mission. We launched with a command module full of instruments, many of which we had never seen before. They handed us the checklist kind of on the way in and said 'Good luck, guys.'"

As they rendezvoused with the stricken *Skylab*, astronauts Joe Kerwin and Pete Conrad climbed out of their *Apollo* capsule, hoping to repair the broken sun panel by hand.

Above: **The damaged *Skylab* sun panel.**

"It was in an area of the spacecraft where there were no handrails, and there were some sharp edges," Kerwin says. "When we finally pried that solar panel up and the hinge which had been frozen suddenly loosened, Conrad and I both went flying head over heels into outer space. We were pulled up sharply when our tethers stretched out, and we just hand-over-handed ourselves back to the nearest thing we could grab onto. Then we could turn around and look back up and see that solar panel cover sitting fully erected. That was one of the prettiest sights I've ever seen."

Salvaging *Skylab* led to three long-term stays for American astronauts in space. They inhabited *Skylab* for 171 straight days, a new record for manned space flight.

But solar flares inter- fered with *Skylab's* orbit, and lack of fund- ing grounded future missions. In 1979, NASA pulled the plug. America's first space station plunged into the seas off Australia.

Right: Skylab as it headed back to Earth.

As work on the International Space Station began, NASA was aware of the challenges. "With the space station, we're going to have to learn in space. And when things go wrong, the astronauts out in space are going to have to figure out what to do," chief administrator Daniel S. Goldin says. "The space station is like a submarine under the polar ice cap. If you have a fire or a collision, you have to deal with it on the spot, and you can't go back and ask for help."

Back on Endeavour, *the first of many space walks that will be made to build the International Space Station goes well. The shuttle's crew flips the switches, and the nucleus of the station comes to life. Humanity has taken a major step towards building a habitat for living in space. But living in space may prove to be the biggest challenge of all.*

In 1986, the Soviet Union launched its second space station. Its name was *Mir*, which means "peace" in Russian. The new Soviet spacecraft was the

Left and right: Mir space station in orbit around Earth.

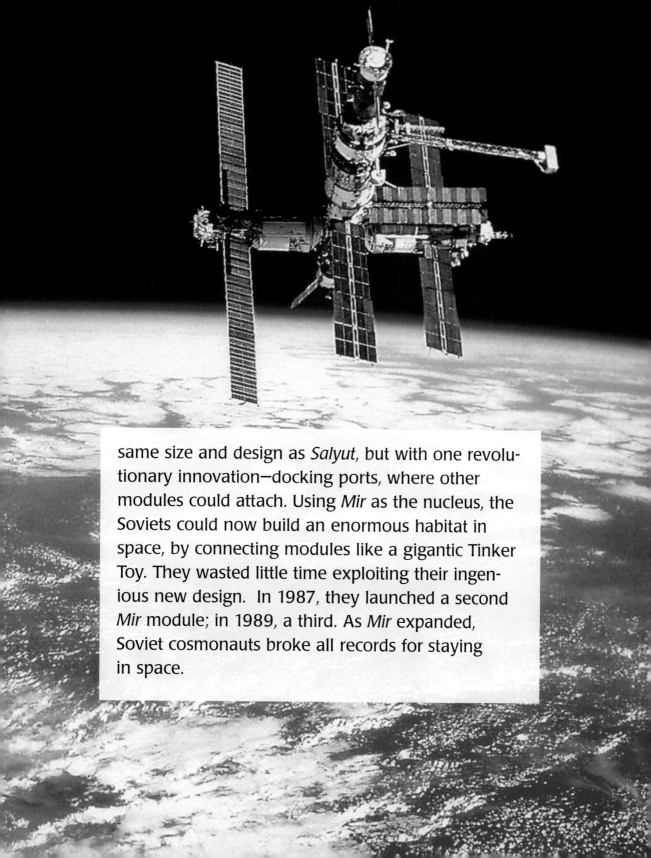

same size and design as *Salyut*, but with one revolutionary innovation—docking ports, where other modules could attach. Using *Mir* as the nucleus, the Soviets could now build an enormous habitat in space, by connecting modules like a gigantic Tinker Toy. They wasted little time exploiting their ingenious new design. In 1987, they launched a second *Mir* module; in 1989, a third. As *Mir* expanded, Soviet cosmonauts broke all records for staying in space.

Right: President Ronald Reagan ordered NASA to develop a space station to compete with *Mir*.

Right: The collapse of the Soviet Union in 1991 crippled the Soviet space program and offered new opportunities to NASA.

Opposite: U.S. astronaut John Blaha was one of the first Americans to live aboard *Mir*.

America tried to compete. In the 1980's, President Ronald Reagan ordered NASA to design a new space station, *Freedom*. Its astronomical cost was to be shared by America's allies, including Canada, Britain, and Japan. Yet the knowledge gap between NASA and its Russian counterparts was huge. The Soviets seemed destined to dominate the quest to live in space.

But the Soviets' dreams came crashing down to Earth, as their economy and political system collapsed. After the breakup of the Soviet Union in 1991, the Russian space program struggled on, blessed with unparalleled technical knowledge, cursed by an utter lack of funds. America had plenty of money, but little expertise in building or operating space stations. It didn't take long for the two old enemies to rethink their relationship. By 1995, American astronauts were living in

space with the cosmonauts of *Mir*, and Russian engineers had become partners in building the *Freedom*, now officially renamed the International Space Station.

As Americans began living on *Mir*, they soon discovered that the flagship of life in space was not all it seemed to be.

American astronaut John Blaha, who lived aboard *Mir* for over one hundred days in 1996 and 1997, has never forgotten his first impressions: "On the inside, four of the six modules looked like a well-used garage, with lots of spare parts stuck all over the walls, in drawers, anywhere you could put them. My initial reaction was, 'Wow, this is small, it is cramped, and what is that bad odor?'"

Blaha's successor, Jerry Linenger, pulled no punches in a live television tour of *Mir*, broadcast to Earth in May, 1997, pointing out rust caused by condensation and other signs of deterioration. By that time, *Mir* had been in space for eleven years and was showing its age. Its

crew had struggled with leaky coolant systems, corroded pipes, and, on February 23, a frightening flash fire. Linenger described how a flame had shot through the space station, burning for fourteen minutes.

After giving his TV tour, Linenger was relieved by a new American astronaut, Michael Foal. Just weeks after that, another accident almost killed Foal and the two Russian cosmonauts aboard *Mir*.

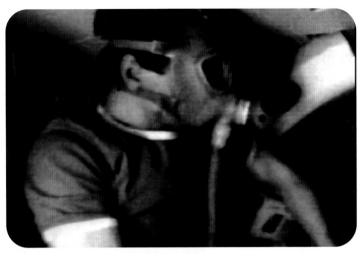

Opposite: Inside *Mir*, parts and equipment made for cluttered conditions.

Above: emergency oxygen masks were needed after the fire on board *Mir*.

Left: Jerry Linenger points to rust and corrosion inside the *Mir* modules.

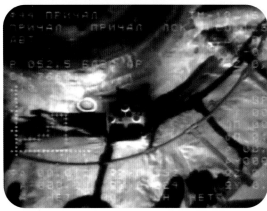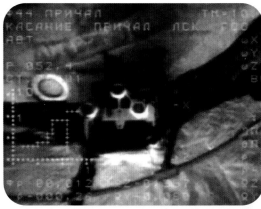

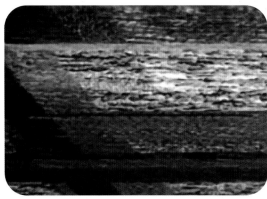

On June 25th, 1997, Russian ground controllers told *Mir's* commander to dock the module with an orbiting supply ship, using a difficult new procedure. The commander complained that he was too tired, but the controllers ordered him to proceed. What happened next remains controversial. However it happened, the supply ship collided with a *Mir* module, punching a hole in the hull.

Mir began to depressurize. It lost 15 percent of its air pressure before the crew found a way to temporarily seal off the leaking compartment

and save the ship. For about 15 minutes, *Mir* seemed doomed.

Mir's woes taught Russia and America a sobering lesson: Living in space would not be easy. But the beleaguered habitat also provided a treasure trove of new data about space life, and ingeniously simple solutions to some of its fundamental problems. For example, on *Mir*, water vapor was taken out of the air, run through a cleaning system, and used to produce seven or eight liters of pure drinking water every day.

Opposite: **This sequence shows the supply ship (above) approach and collision with *Mir*.**

"People looked at the warts and blemishes of *Mir* and thought of the Russians as having a broken down program," says Daniel S. Goldin. "But this vessel traveled a farther distance than any other vessel in the history of the human species. Not one life was lost, and there was not one serious medical injury to anyone."

December 10, 1998

Space shuttle commander Robert Cabana and Russian cosmonaut Sergei Krikalev carefully open the air lock connecting the shuttle Endeavour *with the modules* Unity *and* Zarya. *They are exhilarated to enter and become the first inhabitants of the International Space Station. But space veterans like Krikalev and Cabana know that spending a few days in orbit is one thing, and living there is another.*

Prolonged space flight has some disturbing side effects. Returning to Earth after four months on *Mir*, John Blaha tried to unbuckle his seat belt and got an unpleasant surprise.

"My hand never made it to the belt buckle. It was literally slammed back down, into the floor," Blaha recalls. "I felt like there was this huge magnet that was pulling me to the center of the Earth—so much so that when I was lying in a bed ten hours later, in the crew quarters, I felt like I was going to get sucked right through the mattress."

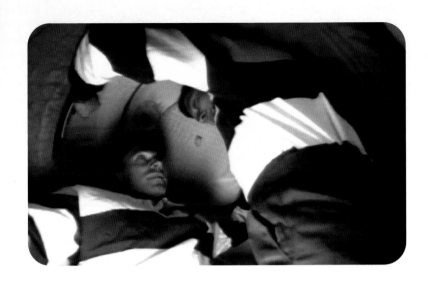

Left: Cabana and Krikalev open the air lock that connected *Endeavour* to *Unity* and *Zarya*.

Below: The *Endeavour* returning to Earth.

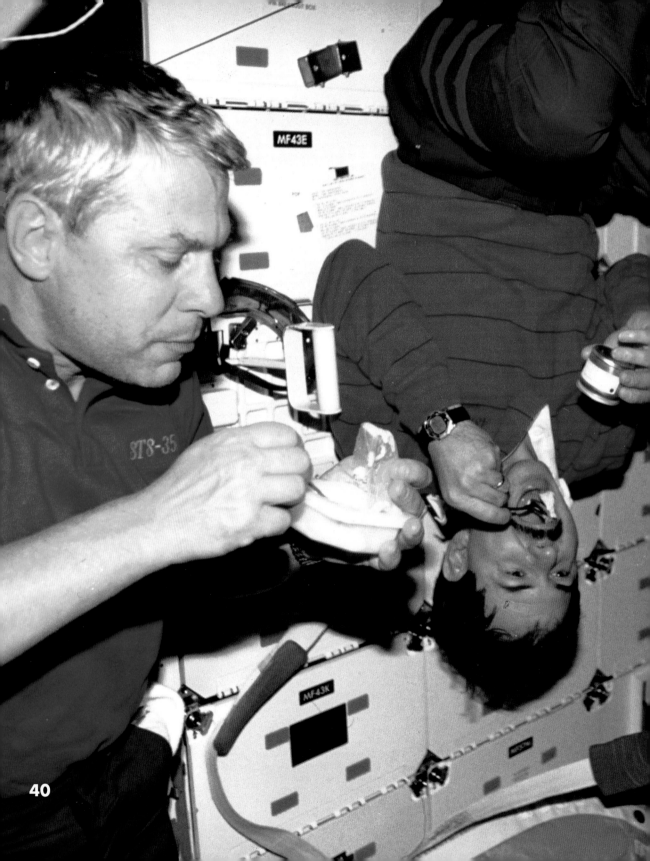

Blaha's muscles had shrunk. He had lost 10 percent of the soft bone tissue in his hip joint. He needed six months of physical therapy to recover.

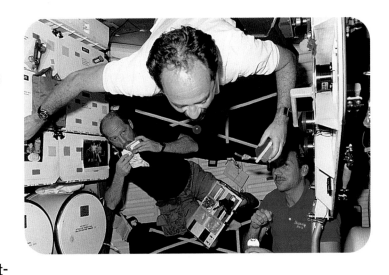

Escaping gravity may seem like the most fun anyone could have in space. But floating effortlessly for months or years is not what our bodies evolved to do. To combat muscle and bone loss and maintain their cardiovascular systems, space station dwellers will have to exercise vigorously. But exercise only retards physical deterioration—it cannot prevent it. If we intend to live in space, we must find a way to conquer the crippling effects of prolonged weightlessness.

At NASA's Ames Research Center in Mountainview, California, scientists are pondering the problems of microgravity. In the future, humans may live for years on the station, doing scientific research and training for voyages to Mars. No one knows what will happen to people

Opposite and above: **NASA researchers must find ways to help humans survive while in weightlessness for long periods of time.**

deprived for so long of the invisible force that controls almost everything they do. Gravity controls how you move, how your face looks—in orbit, cheeks puff out as fluid builds up in the face. Gravity even con-

trols the shape of the retina, so that in space, astronauts see differently than they do on Earth.

Microgravity even affects the way crewmembers interact. Without clear up-and-down orientation, it can be hard to distinguish a smile from a grimace or even a frown. That makes communication tougher. The fact that the space station is manned by international crews adds to the problem, as does the stress of long space flights.

"There definitely is something that happens to human beings on long duration space flight, psychologically," says Blaha. "On *Mir*, I really felt that I was separated from Earth, in a way that I'll never forget."

"I felt *Mir* was my new planet, and Valeri and Sasha, the two cosmonauts who were with me, were the only human beings that lived on this planet. But about two weeks into the mission, I said to myself 'John, something's not the same here for you.'"

John Blaha was suffering from depression. When he returned to Earth, he described his experience to psychiatrists who investigate how space flight affects the mind.

One theory is that some of the psychological factors that occur during long space flights result from being

Opposite and left: Exercise in space is critical for maintaining muscle mass. Here, inhabitants of Mir and the space station train aboard the ship.

in a microgravity environment, in which the nervous system is understimulated. On long missions, too, monotony sets in. People begin to get territorial; they get tired of hearing the same old stories; they irritate each other. The ability to deal with other people in a difficult environment becomes as important as the ability to handle tasks and crises.

While scientists grapple with the problems of space travel, NASA administrators must deal with difficulties on Earth. Some critics have questioned the space station's multi-billion dollar expense, especially the millions paid to its struggling co-builder, Russia. NASA officials admit the space station is expensive and controversial, but they also call it "the indispensable first step towards our intergalactic future."

"We intend to leave Earth orbit," says Daniel Goldin. "Americans and our partners are bold, and we intend to explore our solar system and then ultimately our universe. You cannot prepare to leave Earth by doing research on the ground. The only place we're going to do that is in space."

Researchers and scientists say that the space station will allow humans to begin a journey that will lead to exploration of the universe.

With every year that goes by, the space station is faced with solving new and often dangerous problems. After the space shuttle *Columbia* exploded on February 1, 2003, three U.S. astronauts–scheduled to return to Earth–were stranded in the space station indefinitely. It wasn't until late April 2003 that a quickly organized Russian *Soyuz* mission could be launched to bring new astronauts to replace the stranded crew. The *Soyuz* successfully docked with the space station on April 28, in what NASA deputy administrator, Frederick Gregory, called "a beautiful docking."

"The International Space Station partnership has been tested by a great challenge," Gregory said. "The partnership has risen to the challenge and demonstrated that we are able to overcome any obstacle on the road to the future."

Like all great undertakings, the International Space Station faces frightening risks and daunting challenges. Yet if we can build this super structure in space, we may someday achieve our age-old dream of voyaging to the stars. Millennia from now, it may still be remembered as one of the great achievements of the human species.

Glossary

aeronautics science that deals with flight and aircraft

aviator a person who operates an aircraft

beleaguered troubled

cardiovascular having to do with the heart and blood vessels

components parts

crew a team of people in an aircraft or ship

flagship the first or most important aircraft or ship in a series

ground controller a person who directs the movements of an aircraft from the ground

habitat environment

lynchpin a piece that holds together a larger structure

microgravity weightlessness; almost complete absence of gravity

millennium a period of one thousand years

module a part of a space vehicle that can be operated separately

rendezvous a process in which two spacecraft are brought together

solar panel a spacecraft's battery made up of solar cells

INDEX